SURVIVING

CANCER

*The Healing Power of
Faith, Prayer, and
Storytelling*

TORIE PEEKS ANDERSON

WESTBOW
PRESS®
A DIVISION OF THOMAS NELSON
& ZONDERVAN

This book is a work of non-fiction. Unless otherwise noted, the author and the publisher make no explicit guarantees as to the accuracy of the information contained in this book and in some cases, names of people and places have been altered to protect their privacy.

Scripture quotations taken from The Holy Bible, New International Version® NIV® Copyright © 1973 1978 1984 2011 by Biblica, Inc. TM. Used by permission. All rights reserved worldwide.

Scripture quotations taken from the New American Standard Bible®, Copyright © 1960, 1962, 1963, 1968, 1971, 1972, 1973, 1975, 1977, 1995 by The Lockman Foundation. Used by permission. (www.Lockman.org)

WestBow Press books may be ordered through booksellers or by contacting:

WestBow Press
A Division of Thomas Nelson & Zondervan
1663 Liberty Drive
Bloomington, IN 47403
www.westbowpress.com
844-714-3454

Because of the dynamic nature of the Internet, any web addresses or links contained in this book may have changed since publication and may no longer be valid. The views expressed in this work are solely those of the author and do not necessarily reflect the views of the publisher, and the publisher hereby disclaims any responsibility for them.

Any people depicted in stock imagery provided by Getty Images are models, and such images are being used for illustrative purposes only. Certain stock imagery © Getty Images.

ISBN: 979-8-3850-1115-5 (sc)
ISBN: 979-8-3850-1113-1 (hc)
ISBN: 979-8-3850-1114-8 (e)

Library of Congress Control Number: 2023920565

Print information available on the last page.

WestBow Press rev. date: 10/31/2023

To my Christian family at Immanuel Baptist Church,
who has supported me in growing closer to God and
carried me through many uncertain times.

This is a story about the faithfulness of God when worldly hope is gone and darkness raises its ugly head. The value of close friends sharing during your trying times can be a better medicine than what one can find in an IV tube.

CONTENTS

CONTENTS

AUTHOR'S NOTE

It's no secret that laughter and uplifting stories can have healing effects on the body (*Sunwolf, Storytelling, Self, Society,* vol. 1, no.2, 2005). The link between the mind and the body is powerful. Humor and laughter have been found to release endorphins that make us feel good. They can strengthen our immune system, reduce stress, and actually increase our tolerance to pain (PyschCentral, October 5, 2021).

Storytelling has been known to break through the barriers of depression, anxiety, and stress which causes the limbic system of the brain to pull blood and oxygen away from our neocortex. When stressed, our heart rate increases, and our adrenal gland secretes the stress hormone cortisol into the blood. This prepares us for a possible flight-or-fight situation in order to protect ourselves (J. Diane Connell, *Brain-Based Strategies to Reach Every Learner*). We tense up and can't relax. Our mind freezes and our bodies tend to shut down.

As a teacher dealing with students suffering from post-traumatic stress syndrome, I had to attend to their sense of well-being before they were ready to learn academics. Making them feel safe and comfortable in our classroom-learning environment helped them attend their lessons. Telling stories they enjoyed formed a unity in our class, plus it helped form positive relationships between the students and myself. Children with ADHD tendencies were calmer and more focused when placed in situations where they experienced a calm orderly environment and received positive feedback. Storytelling breaks the ice.

One of the first things my doctor told me when I realized I had fibromyalgia was to reduce my stress levels. When under stress, I experienced more pain and cognitive deficiencies. Listening to music, hearing and reading stories, and writing in my journal were very relaxing. I felt better and I was more functional. I felt May Lin would benefit in the same ways while battling cancer.

I was inspired to write this story because my prayer list of people with cancer kept growing and growing. As I have reached my golden years, I see more and more incidents of cancer around me. According to the American Cancer Society, that's to be expected as we age. People have told me that the cure is worse than the disease, and death can look like a welcome relief. But what I've found to be true is that those who pray and lean on God for healing have a better chance of surviving than those who rely on medical treatments alone.

People of faith have a whole book of promises from God that have been tried and proved throughout the ages. Jesus asked, "Shall I not drink the cup My Father has given Me?" (John 18:11).

Doing God's will and thereby experiencing suffering, as did Christ, is the highest form of faith and the most glorious Christian achievement.

We are not left without hope, for we are being prepared for our eternal future. Our work is to lay our petitions before the Lord, and in childlike simplicity to pour out our hearts before Him, saying, "I do not deserve that You should you hear me and answer my requests, but for the sake of my precious Lord Jesus; answer my prayer. And give me the grace to wait patiently until it pleases You to grant my petition. For I believe You will do it in Your own time and way!" (L. B. Cowman, *Streams in the Desert*).

More prayer, more exercising of our faith, and more patient waiting lead to blessings—abundant blessings. I have found it to be true throughout my sixty years of following Christ.

ENDORSEMENTS

My relationship with Torie Anderson began when we first met in 1968 at California Baptist College. It was clear even in those early years that she was passionate about becoming a teacher for special needs children, which had grown out of her witnessing the abuse and bullying of her younger mentally impaired brother.

Torie married my roommate Bob Anderson in 1970. They have one son who lives nearby. Throughout their marriage, they have traveled around the world. While visiting third-world countries, Torie felt convicted that she could use her teaching skills to help improve the lives she encountered. God gave her that opportunity when China experienced a 7.9 earthquake in the Sichuan Province on May 12, 2008. She joined a faith-based team called Partners in Development Worldwide with members from China, Canada, and the United States as they gave humanitarian and counseling aid to the earthquake victims.

I met Ken, May Lin's husband, many years ago while I was a pastor and ministering to the prayer needs of the employees where Ken worked. He had met a Chinese girl online and developed a relationship with her which took him to China to meet her parents and eventually got married. Ken and May Lin attended my church, and when Torie was looking for someone to accompany her to China, I introduced them. While in China, they helped Torie with language interpretation and the logistics of giving educational conferences.

Their relationship grew, and they have remained close friends since then. As with all Christian testimonies, they need to be shared so others will be encouraged to stay faithful to Christ in times of difficulty. This story is a testimony of that kind of faith and a righteous example of true friendship and love. Jesus gave us an example to follow. Once tested and proved in the Refiner's Fire (Malachi 3:2, NIV), there is no limit to how God can use a faithful servant.

Rev. K. Galen Greenwalt
Senior pastor
Earlsboro Baptist Church, Oklahoma
Used by permission

October 19, 2022

Torie Anderson is an amazing woman who has a heart for God, who follows Him and serves her Lord to her greatest ability. Torie joined Immanuel Baptist Church in 1992. She has been a faithful member and has a great heart for missions.

As you read her book you will see what I am talking about. It will move you and inspire you at the same time. May the Lord be praised and blessed as we all strive to be a blessing to someone else in this journey of life. Torie is a blessing to be cherished, and I pray her book will be a blessing to you!

To God be the Glory
Pastor Dr. Rob Zinn
Immanuel Baptist Church
Used by permission

February 2, 2023

Torie and I were teaching partners for eleven years in Kindergarten. I was new to that age group, having taught fifth and sixth grade, so it was with reservations that I agreed to teach the younger children. I told Torie when we started, "I don't do puppets." She laughed and eased me into my new role with great patience and skill.

I first met Torie in 1985 when she was teaching fifth grade, and I was a new teacher also to fifth grade. Our principal paired us up so Torie could mentor me, and after that, our colleagues said we were "joined at the hip." However, we were also joined spiritually. As Christians, we embedded biblical principles into our lessons, teaching morals and values to our students. Our families have traveled to many places together and have enjoyed adventures most people would try to avoid. It's been an incredible journey for the two of us.

For the glory of our Lord,
Kim Williams
Fifth-grade teacher
Myers Elementary School
Used by permission

In 2009, at Immanuel Baptist church, I attended a presentation regarding an opportunity to participate in serving on an educational mission team to China. The charismatic presenter described the specific details regarding educational needs in Chinese schools. I was so impressed and spiritually motivated to meet this dynamic presenter to share my interest and willingness to join her mission team! It was at this meeting that I first met Torie Anderson.

Torie and I served on many educational mission trips to China. She is highly respected and appreciated by Chinese educational leaders, teachers, and students! It is evident that Torie loves the Lord with all her heart, soul, mind, and strength. The Lord has truly gifted her with a passion and compassion for the Chinese educational community. I have witnessed Torie speak to assemblies of large captivated audiences, and at the same meetings, I've witnessed her speak so tenderly with inquiring individuals. Torie is truly a gift to all who come in contact with her!

As I read the true life story of *Surviving Cancer*, I was so personally touched by Torie's open heart and unconditional love for May Lin. Upon reading her story, you too will experience the potency of God's spirit, the love Torie expresses to May Lin, and God's divine provision to his children. It's a blessing to know and see how God is using Torie through life's journey.

Art Gallardo
Retired school principal
San Bernardino Unified School District
Used by permission

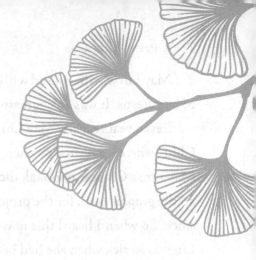

Chapter 1

THE DIAGNOSIS

Never be afraid to trust an unknown to an unknown God.
—Corrie Ten Boom

October, 2015

May Lin began experiencing pain in her lower abdomen. She ignored it for as long as she could, but when the pain increased, she finally saw a doctor. Suspecting cancer, the doctor said she needed to have exploratory surgery.

January 28, 2016

May Lin was in surgery for six hours instead of the original four-hour window of time her doctor said it would take to do the surgery. Sondra Greenwalt, a mutual close friend, and I sat with her husband Ken and watched the doctor walk toward us. We knew the news was not good.

May Lin was diagnosed with cervical cancer which had spread to her uterus. It was an aggressive form of cancer.

Seven years earlier, May Lin and Ken had accompanied me to China where I, a retired teacher, was giving education conferences. May Lin, a Chinese national, did the translations for me. Ken did all the graphic work for the projects. We've been close friends ever since. So when I heard this news, it was hard to believe that May Lin was so sick when she had been so healthy and vibrant.

The doctor said May Lin had the worst case of endometriosis she had ever seen in her entire career. She couldn't understand how May Lin could have endured the pain for so long before seeing a doctor. It took her all those hours to pull apart tangled scar tissues growing outside her uterus and throughout her female organs and the intestine leading to the rectum.

In the midst of all that was cancer. Besides surgery, May Lin would also need to do a series of chemotherapy and radiation treatments, and if the cancer was still there, then there was little else to be done but to help make May Lin comfortable. Since the cancer was so advanced, the doctor was pessimistic, and she didn't want to give us false hope!

However, as a child, I often gazed upon the clouds after a storm and marveled at the rainbow which appeared bright and colorful across the sky. I grew up witnessing the power of God in His handiwork, and I concluded that if He could make rainbows form out of angry clouds and a dark sky, He could bring healing to a broken body. May Lin and I had experienced the power of God in other areas of our lives, and we knew God had a plan and purpose for putting us through the trials we faced.

Our hope was not only in the medical procedures. Our hope was also based on the power of the One who makes rainbows.

Chapter 2

THE HEALING JOURNEY

I will make all my mountains into roads.
—Isaiah 49:11

Sondra had to return to her home in Oklahoma. Since I lived a one and a half hour's drive away from Ken and May Lin, I rented a room close to their condo so I could help her recuperate at home. After a week, I came home but tried to visit May Lin every weekend. She was so pale, thin, and weak. But she and Ken always came out and met me at the door with smiles.

We would spend the afternoons reading the Bible and praying. Her prayers were earnest and passionate, not about herself but about her family, friends, and the world. She never blamed God for her condition but surprisingly praised him.

I was struggling with my own health issues which eventually kept me from visiting May Lin as much as I wanted to, so we relied on emails and phone calls, thus began the storytelling, restoring the mind and spirit. Jesus told stories (parables) to aid in helping people understand His messages. May Lin and I told stories to aid in our understanding of God's providence in our lives. Whenever I seek answers for life's perils, I look to God's natural design of creation, and many times the nuggets of wisdom are there.

March 2

Dear May Lin,

Yes, this is much easier than texting on the phone. I can type more easily than I can tap. Ha! I'm very happy, and I'm praising God that you are doing so well.

I'm finding particular comfort in the book of Isaiah. I wish time would allow me to study it more deeply. I think even if the rest of the Bible was not there, we could know what we need to know to obey and trust God. We can know his plan of salvation. We can learn about the coming of Jesus, why He came, what He was to suffer, how He was to suffer, His crucifixion, resurrection, and his reign over a new heaven and new earth (Isaiah).

Isaiah identifies sin, the trappings of sin, and what he considers most important to him. Over and over again, He emphasizes the Lord's compassion for the poor, the sick, the widows, the orphans, and those oppressed by the lack of justice.

"The Lord will guide you always; he will satisfy your needs in a sun-scorched land and will strengthen your frame. You will be like a well-watered garden, like a spring whose waters never fail" (Isaiah 58:11, NIV).

I love that analogy. I can visualize a beautiful garden with colorful flowers immersed in springs of bubbling water and waterfalls pouring into a lake where graceful swans glide proudly. We will be strengthened, nourished, refreshed, and deeply cared for just like those swans.

Heavenly Father, we ask for healing from the living waters of Your word. Thank You for allowing us to share in Your suffering to experience Your compassion and mercy as You guide us along this journey that we don't understand. But we trust You to bring us where we need to be in our relationship with You. We know nothing happens by chance, and You have a purpose behind our circumstances. We claim this living water for healing so our bodies and our spirits will be just as beautiful and alluring to nonbelievers as a beautiful garden.

In Tennessee, where I was born, my grandmother drew water from a mountain spring most of the days of her life. She adhered to the "old ways" even though she could access modern conveniences. Lantern light glowed through her windows at night. She cooked on a wood-burning stove and fetched water from a spring near her roughly built wooden house, which had been home for her eleven children.

The water was so sweet, clear, and refreshing. It was hidden by vines and bushes growing around it. We'd have to push back the foliage to see it. But you could hear its trickle as the tiny stream of water made its long journey down the mountain into the little hole at the side of the road, so small on the outside but deep in volume underground. No one could figure out just how deep the spring was, but it didn't matter. The water it produced refreshed generations past and would do so for generations to come. Even when the county paved Hollar Road, great care was taken not to disturb the spring.

Our spiritual lives are like that. Christ in us is "living water" (John 4:10, NIV). Only God knows how deep our commitment is to Him, but others can reap the benefits of the service we do in His name.

So dear May Lin, let's think of ourselves today as a well-watered garden. Visualize the colors and fragrance of flowers, the different shades of green, the grand stature of the trees. Bees are buzzing a comforting hum, and butterflies are flitting around us giving delicate kisses on the flowers. Humming birds serenade us with their songs. And visualize the sun with its light and warmth like the love and protection of our Lord Jesus.

We are blessed! Thank you, dear Lord, for being all You are when we are not all we are. You complete us.

In love, we pray,

Torie

March 3

Dear precious sister Torie,

As I told you over the phone, I could see clearly the beauty of the Lord's gifts inside you to describe, to denote, to deliver the beautiful things God has shown you.

I even copied/pasted part of your email: your childhood memory of your grandma's hidden mountain spring and the analogy you used about our spiritual garden abiding in the Lord. I sent it to one of my old friends, who like you, keeps praying for me during this trial.

I love this visualized garden analogy you shared with me. Every day, I come to realize how amazingly our physical body has been designed, created, maintained, managed, nurtured, cared for, and protected by our faithful heavenly Father through His Son's blood, and via the wonderful work of His spirit.

I do believe in a spiritual sphere; our body is being continuously cleansed, washed, and nourished by the powerful loving hand of God through our daily circumstances. His Holy Spirit will testify this to our spirit when our heart is seeking Him in His Word.

I am very pleased to have a sister like you to share this hidden sweet water with me in His spirit to encourage me to pour out all my heart, to be confident and bold to run toward our Father rather than to run away from Him, to let the Lord fill me up to know Him more intimately and to do His will more faithfully and patiently and let His Holy Spirit flow freely through me to nurture more souls for His kingdom.

Love in His gardening spirit and the
nourishing name of Jesus Christ!
May Lin

March 4

You are very kind, May Lin. Thank you for the nice compliments; but we know where all our talents and gifts come from. I don't have time right now to send you our next scriptures. I had been at church most of the day, and later, I went to visit a friend in the hospital. I give you all the credit for the inspiration you gave me to write these things. We are a team whom God has brought together "for such a time as this" (Esther 4:14) and for His glory. Isn't it exciting to think about what He has planned for us? Have a peaceful restful night.

Love you,
Torie

March 6

Dear May Lin,

I love the picture you sent me of your little ducks. It's so appropriate for our discussion. As they say, "A picture speaks a thousand words." What is it saying? To me, it means that God cares for all His creatures, even little ducklings; and there is always a new life when the old one passes away. The mother duck follows behind, protecting her babies, as God has our back and protects us.

I have another story I'd like to share with you. Let me know if you get tired of hearing my stories.

Because we lived in a wooded area, my father and brother had ample room to hunt. They didn't kill for the fun of it, but we ate what was killed.

If the animal had babies, my dad would bring them home and we raised them as pets. We've raised squirrels and even had a pet owl. We loved animals. My father raised beagle dogs and trained them to go hunting with him.

The one animal I remember the most was a crow. Daddy brought home these two little baby crows still in their nest. He said it had fallen out of the tree, and now the mother would abandon them. My brother, Allen, and I fed them softened bread in milk from a spoon. The small one died, but the other one was strong and lived. Allen named him "Herdie Birdie."

We all loved the crow, but it was attached to Allen. It would ride on his shoulders or arm. It walked behind him and followed him wherever he went. The crow began talking, imitating my mother when she yelled at my brother who was always getting into mischief, "Allen, come home! Allen, stop playing in the car!"

When my dad and Allen went hunting, the crow rode on Allen's shoulder. It was quite a picture (like something out of Tom Sawyer and Huckleberry Finn novels). Deeply etched in my memory is my dad with his gun slung over his shoulder, Allen walking behind him with his gun, the beagles walking behind with their tails straight up, and my cat (who thought she was a dog) tagging along, traipsing through the forest. I could almost hear the music of Prokofiev's "Peter and the Wolf" playing in the background.

I guess the point I'm making in sharing this story is that a crow was born wild. But because of his association with us and the loving care we gave him, he learned to trust and love us too. Herdie Birdie chose to stay with us even though he could have flown off with other crows. We never clipped his wings as some people suggested.

He left his old identity behind, just like we do when we give ourselves to Christ. We become "new creations" (2 Corinthians 5:17, NIV).

God says, "Peace, peace, to those far and near, and I will heal them" (Isaiah 57:19, NIV).

We are not crows. We are God's beloved children. How much more will He attend to our needs and protect us because we are made in His image?

Loving you,
Torie

March 8

Dear May Lin,

Usually when God removes the old things in our lives (illnesses, the loss of a loved one, job loss, or divorce), it's usually a sign that He is preparing us for a new beginning. The employer where you worked is challenging your right to use your insurance to pay for your medical bills. This is not right, and I see the anguish it causes you and Ken. It's bad enough that you are suffering so much already with this cancer, but to deny the insurance you deserve just shows how evil seeps in to cause more grief. I'm glad you have a lawyer to help you, and I'm sure you will win your case.

Can you imagine never getting a second chance? I don't know how many times I've "blown it" and felt doomed to failure. However, Jesus paid the price for us to have second chances, even seventy times seven. Perhaps the Lord has a better job in mind for you when you are healed. In the meantime, I'll pray for Ken to get plenty of work.

I remember my father had a difficult time finding a job after WWII. The government provided some work through a program called the Tennessee Valley Authority (TVA) which built hydroelectric dams to bring electricity to seven states, including my small hometown, Elizabethton. But once the dams were built the work ran out; so we had to move to a place where my dad could find a job. He got a second chance, and he thanked God for it.

My father had a quiet inner faith he didn't share with other people. He went to church occasionally, and one time, I remember him kneeling with the pastor and praying with him. Sometimes I saw him reading his Bible and praying, but it was not enough to drive the evil demons away that haunted him. Some blamed it on the war, some blamed it on his upbringing, but whatever it was caused episodes of violent anger. We never knew what would set him off. One time, we were eating dinner. My dad was unusually quiet. Then, without saying a word, he swiped all the dishes off the table and onto the floor. Sometimes my mother came and slept with me because my dad would have horrible nightmares. I could hear him moaning and screaming into the night.

PTS (post-traumatic stress) was unheard of at the time. There was no help for soldiers returning home from the horrors of war. Veterans were told, "Get over it, move on" without counseling on how to do it.

My dad had to leave Elizabethton and look for work on his own before sending for my mother. He found work for both of them at a manufacturing company in Maryland about 500 miles away from our hometown. I remember my mother, little brother, and I caught a Greyhound bus to Maryland in the middle of the night. Allen was small enough to sit in my mother's lap. The bus was crowded, and people were grumpy and irritable. I had a little blue doll trunk with my clothes in it that sat out in the aisle for lack of room to store it anywhere else. I was four years old and I loved to sing. I knew the lyrics of most country music songs. I don't know what gave me the notion, but I sat down on the chest and bellowed out, "Hey, good-lookin', what you got cookin'? How about cookin' somethin' up for me?"

People stopped talking and just stared. I continued with "I got a hot rod Ford and a two-dollar bill. And I know a spot right over the hill. There's soda pop and the dancing's free. So if you wanna have fun, come along with me ..."

By that time the whole bus was singing even the driver. Perhaps it was an omen of things to come because I used the same audacity when I worked in China as a teacher. Being the oldest, I was more independent and daring than my younger brother. I didn't analyze what I should do but just followed my instinct.

Now, I believe it was the Holy Spirit coaxing me early on to act outside my comfort zone. As always, He knows our future. As I looked closely at my past, I found lots of clues where God had His providential hand on all the phases of my life. The Holy Spirit becomes our teacher and guide. He knew I would be here with you, May Lin, at this time.

Thinking of you,
Torie

March 10

My dear May Lin,

My thoughts are of you and the quest we share to know our God and Savior more deeply.

I praise and thank you, Lord, for giving me books on the power of prayer, fasting, and spiritual warfare. I believe, Father, that You endow Christians with the gift of taking Your word and giving practical insights into its meaning and application. Reading the testimonies of people who have gone through similar experiences as we are facing now, encourages and inspires me to keep my focus on the task You have put before me.

I'm coming to understand, beloved sister, God wants to do more than just heal our bodies. We are His greatest instrument to give Him glory and win others to Christ. God seldom uses *things* to accomplish His will. He uses *people*. He must have someone to use as a conduit for the Holy Spirit. Jesus said, that from within Him, "Shall flow rivers of living waters" (John 4:10, NIV).

I don't know what you are feeling physically right now, but I pray that whatever you are experiencing will not be used by Satan to weaken your faith and your focus on God. Through the strength of the power of Christ, I am beginning to praise and thank Him for the pain I'm experiencing from my illness. We are sharing in the sufferings of Jesus. In a way, each pain is praise to Jesus because he is taking the time to teach us some important things. I am weak but He is strong. This is my cross and it must be borne graciously, so the Lord will be glorified. And as Jesus defeated the cross and was resurrected, we can also have that assurance of resurrection to a new life with a perfect new body. Renewed, refreshed, cleansed of all sin, and clothed in the righteousness of Christ is our future.

Have a good day. Let me know what you are feeling.

Love,
Torie

March 19

Dear loving sister Torie,

Thank you for your faithful checking and praying, and I'm sorry for not having responded to you quickly due to my energy level limitation. I will try to respond and share more when I can later. Now, I would like to report to you what happened during my second chemo treatment, which was done on March 14.

During the chemo,

1. overall, it went peacefully, no choking, no flashing lights;
2. I felt tightness in my heart and chest pain, making it hard to breathe; and
3. the in-charge nurse behaved unkindly, and gave me the "cold shoulder." I think she got impatient with me because I asked many questions. I did not fight back but just prayed for her to have patience and kindness. As a patient, the nurse's attitude means a great deal to me and I feel is most important because sick people need to be around others who are positive.

After the chemo,

1. the obvious side effects are nausea and the irritating generated saliva;
2. getting easily fatigued is another symptom; I felt drugged out for four days after the chemo; and
3. the skin pain in the belly and scalp and bone pain in my lower back and legs are issues, besides the numbness in my hands and feet.

Praise report

1. Still no throwing up but I keep eating small things as I can. Still have bowel movements and normal urine.
2. Still I am able to walk every day, indoors and outdoors.
3. Got my wig on March 15. Due to limited options, my wig color is "sun-kissed blonde." I will show you in the coming days.

Prayer requests

1. Let the Lord sustain and order all my blood cells, bowels, bladder, urine, and cervix in the same good condition as He created and managed them.
2. Ask the Holy Spirit to help keep Ken and me in a self-disciplined healthy lifestyle mode in terms of sleeping, eating, drinking, and exercising.
3. Let the Word of God speak to Ken and me and enable us to seek Him, know Him, and rejoice in Him more and more.
4. May God, the Father, show Ken His Sonship's identity in Christ to build up his confidence and set him free from Satan's lies that tell him he is too old and too unqualified to have a job to glorify God.
5. And pray to maintain our health insurance.

Thank you for your prayers, which have been holding us strongly in the love of the Lord and have been enabling me to keep praying for you and your family as well.

Love in Him,
May Lin

March 25

I wrote May Lin yesterday. I had been traveling to her condo where she lives, which is almost two hours travel time away from my home; however, my own health problems were making that difficult. We decided to call and text each other instead. No matter what we were facing, May Lin kept bringing my focus back to the goodness of God.

You know what, Torie, I was just reading your email with the story about your pet crow Herdie Birdie, and I was ready to respond to that one, but then you shot this latest email to me. So I decided to respond to this one instead.

I really love reading the stories you share with me every time we communicate. They are so vividly described and remembered and are all associated with nature, which we both love to explore. I keep seeking the Lord's heart for me, pursuing God's will for my life, and the guidance of the Holy Spirit in this uncertain journey.

Attached are more pictures of the ducklings and baby koi fish in a small pond right outside my door. I just took them today, which for me demonstrates a new energy of life, and God's sovereign protection over them. I do not have the energy or the courage or the wisdom to analyze why I got this cancer now. I know many Christians who suffer illness, but it is not for us to second-guess God and ask why. My desire to seek the Lord's purpose for me is growing. I pursue HIs power in even the basic living things of my life like breathing, sleeping, eating, drinking, tasting, walking, chewing, swallowing, smelling, and hearing ... Every part of me is dependent on my heavenly Father.

I've been expecting to do "big" and "great" things for God for a long time. I have been very dissatisfied and disappointed with my life here in America, in terms of my inability to have children, having a home church, career, friendships, etc. I've been asking myself if I have made a huge mistake by coming to this country and marrying Ken. But now, I tell myself that I must stop thinking this way. God has a purpose for me being here in these circumstances.

Even if I have made poor choices in the past, God has the power to work out everything for our good and for His glory. I know I used to be pretty wild in some ways. In China, I didn't think about religious things. I had my own plans to be successful by any means. I wanted independence to follow the desires of my flesh. Maybe I was born that way or I was influenced by my family or maybe I developed my wildness during my adolescent years.

Yet nothing is hidden from His eyes. He's been watching over me since before I was formed. In the womb, He knew me (Jeremiah 1:5).

I will keep seeking. I will continue pursuing His heart, His mind, and His Spirit. Actually, I believe that's not me who is doing the seeking. But it is Christ who is seeking and continuing to desire me and calling me to Himself. Let's keep encouraged. Let's keep enjoying each other's life stories and journeys together to be closer to the Lord day by day as He is enjoying and drawing us to Him first.

Love you,
May Lin

March 28

Sweet May Lin,

When I read your last email, I was touched so deeply I broke down and cried. You are right. We must remain positive and not think about things we cannot change. Our Lord is our present and future hope and that should remain our main focus. Each day, He is faithful to give me enough energy (as you say), to breathe fresh air, to get out of bed, to eat, and to bask in His love during our quiet times. The fragrance of the honeysuckle growing along my back fence completes these moments of solitude. My senses are aroused by His presence.

I sent you a picture of the birdfeeder I put up in my backyard among my roses. They draw a lot of finches and other small birds. One day, I noticed the birds had filled all the feeding spots on the feeder. Below on the ground, ten to fifteen birds scrambled around for surplus seeds, which had fallen on the ground.

Then I sensed in my spirit the Lord saying, "Watch the birds."

One little bird, instead of feeding itself, started knocking seeds from the feeder to the ground with its bill and feet, so others could eat as well. I thought, *God's provision is manifested in nature to help us understand He will meet all our needs, just like He created these little birds to care for each other.* We can learn so much about God's character by just observing His creation.

If we get too busy to make time with God, then yes, I believe He will cause things to happen to slow us down and to bring our focus back on Him because that's how much He loves us like any Father who loves spending time with his children.

It's like the Lord saying, "Come, let's sit together and visit. Be still and know that I AM God," (Psalm 46:10, NIV).

"But those who hope in the Lord shall renew their strength. They will soar on wings like eagles, they will run and not grow weary, they will walk and not be faint" (Isaiah 40:31, NIV).

I ran off a copy of your email and taped it inside my journal. I gain encouragement when I look back at my previous journal writings and see how God has worked through each phase of my life.

Love,
Torie

April 2

Have you ever heard of Ruth Graham, Billy Graham's wife? She's a remarkable woman, and I've read several of her books. She grew up in China because her parents were missionaries there. Her book *Sitting by My Laughing Fire* has lain on my coffee table for years. I was thinking of tucking it away with other books that I don't read anymore when I felt the spirit urge me to open it up. Her words became my prayers: *Lord, when my soul is weary and my heart is tired and sore, and I have that failing feeling that I can't take anymore; then let me*

know the freshening found in simple childlike prayer,
when the kneeling soul knows surely that a listening
Lord is there.

I sent some pictures to your phone. Two of
the pictures are of my little brother and me when
we were small. The trailer that we lived in was
so small that I had to sleep with my parents, and
Allen slept on the couch. We had no television or
radio, so we would sit in our car at night listening
to country music on the *Grand Old Opera Show.*

We went to bed early because we had to get up
early. My dad would have a bowl of hot cream of
wheat waiting for us when we got up.

Maryland could have some pretty heavy
snowstorms. In 1958, we had over six feet of snow.
My dad carried me on his shoulders, so I wouldn't
get buried beneath the huge drifts. I felt so safe
and secure up there with his hands holding me
tightly. I felt protected and loved.

It's the same feeling I have now. The Lord is
carrying us on His shoulders through this storm.
As you said, "We don't need to know *why* He has
placed us on this journey, but only that He will
carry us through it."

You probably had snow where you lived in the
north of China. My brother and I loved the snow.
For us it meant days off from school, sledding
down hills, having snowball fights, and making

snowmen. For my parents, snow meant roads closed down, frozen water pipes, and loss of days of work. That year my dad had no boots, so mom wrapped old rags around his feet and shoes so he could walk the five miles to the main road and hopefully get a lift into town. If he didn't work, he didn't get paid making money tight.

One day, while my parents were gone, I decided to do them a favor and shovel the snow off their car. It didn't occur to my nine-year-old brain that while I removed the snow, I also removed the paint, which later rusted and turned our car into the ugliest car on the road. My parents were upset, but they didn't punish me because they gave me credit for trying to be helpful. Unfortunately, my dad had to drive around in that car with rust streaks all over it. We couldn't afford a new one. Later, much later, it became a family joke. How so like our Heavenly Father who is so forgiving and has a sense of humor.

Did you ever try to catch snowflakes on your tongue or lie down and make snow angels? We even made ice cream out of it. You don't have to be rich to enjoy life. God gave us nature as a classroom and a playground. What we learn from it and enjoy is much better than what we read in books or store-bought toys. Being sick, I think we are more appreciative of nature because it represents life as ongoing, reliable, constant, and (while at the same time) perpetually changing.

Living in the woods, I've learned how to read some signs of nature. I know fall is approaching when the wild geese fly south for the winter. I wondered, *Who taught them to fly in formation like they do?* And in reverse, I know spring is coming when I see the geese flying north again.

My eyes are growing heavy, so I better get up and move around. It's too early to go to bed.

Heavenly Father, thank You for carrying us on your shoulders when the roads are hard to travel. Thank You that we not only have your Holy Spirit to encourage us to stand strong, but You have given me May Lin to be my spiritual sister to accompany her on her journey and her for mine. I ask, Lord Jesus, that You would eliminate all the side effects of her treatments, so she can eat, sleep, and function to meet her personal daily needs. Thank You for this opportunity to draw nearer to You. We trust You to take us where we need to be and to better glorify you. In Jesus's name, amen!

Please keep me posted on your progress so I can pray accordingly. I love the song "Because He Lives."

Love,
Torie

April 3

Dear May Lin,

I pray you are well enough to enjoy this beautiful day God has given us. I woke up this morning to the sound of the birds chirping their "good morning" song outside my window.

The rain has dampened the air causing it to smell fresh and clean. The mountains and hillsides are such a deep green. It looks like someone spread a carpet of grass over the hills with sprigs of wildflowers peppered throughout the grass, like candy sprinkles on a cake. I can see persistent daisies and poppies nudging their way between the spaces of the rocks as they follow the light from the sun. I am feeling grateful that no matter how I feel physically, I can rest in the assurance that the Lord is faithful to take care of us as He does nature.

The evidence of those assurances is all around us and also in His Word:

1. Psalm 84:1–12 (NIV) (These verses stood out for me.);
2. How lovely is your dwelling place, O Lord Almighty! My soul yearns, even faints, for the courts of the Lord; my heart and my flesh cry out for the Living God (84:1);

3. Even the sparrow has found a home, and the swallow a nest for herself, where she may have her young—a place near your altar, O Lord Almighty my king and my God! (84:3); and

4. Truly, the Lord God is a sun and shield; the Lord bestows favor and honor; no good thing does he withhold from those whose walk is blameless (84:11).

April 5

May Lin,

Easter has always been my favorite time of year. I remember my mother would make sure I was fitted with a new Easter outfit even though money was tight. She would dress my brother and me up and would slip a nickel inside my glove to give for an offering at church. Then she proceeded to take a load of pictures to send to family members in Tennessee.

Before we moved into the country, Allen and I walked to church. For reasons I don't understand, my parents rarely attended church with us. Sometimes, we went to those old tent revivals that were popular in the 1950s. The sawdust would get in my sandals and between my toes. The preacher was loud and condemning. With a long skinny finger, he would point right at me, stare right into my frightened soul (or so it seemed), and ask, "Who does not want to go to hell?"

I made sure I raised my hand.

"Then repent and beg God for His mercy to save you!" he reiterated.

But I wondered, *How do you do that?*

I always loved going to church. The preachers there were much friendlier, and I loved having crafts in Sunday school. Maybe it was because I couldn't attend often, and nobody was forcing me to go, so I always thought of it as a special treat.

All that changed once we moved to the country. The nearest town was fifteen miles away. I could only go to church if my dad felt like taking me or if I could find a ride. Sometimes I would try to bribe him, "Daddy, I'll comb your hair and rub your head fifty times if you will take me to church." (He loved to have his head scratched.)

How are you, dear May Lin? I haven't heard from you for a while.

Love,
Torie

April 6

Dear sister Torie,

I received your old pictures last night and wondered why you sent them at that late hour. Now I know the reason. I hope your EEG test was successful. I will keep praying for that as well.

As usual, your description of your childhood brought so much fun and even beautiful memories. I grew up in the northern part of China which had snow and ice in the winter.

However, I do not have those warm memories you had with your brother and parents. I think that was because my dad was so strict with me and my older brother during our childhood. What we remember most are the early morning exercise training and evening study. Getting a good education and getting into a good school was very important. Our future and the future of our parents depended on it.

I do love snow—its purity, color, and the crunchy sound it makes when you walk on it. Some neighborhood kids made snowmen, and we had snowball fights.

I like the story you recalled where your dad carried you on his shoulder. My big brother would do the same for me if he was in the mood. It made me feel so loved to be scooped up in his arms.

I agree with you that our Lord has been carrying us on His shoulders high and tight when we are too weak and weary to feel, to see, and to use our senses. That's where His spirit will work on each one of us in inexpressible ways through His Word, His children, and even His silence.

Back to my side effects, it's usually hard to cope with right after the chemo. My heart feels tight in my chest which bothers my sleep quality. My stomach and taste buds are messed up, and I have to remind myself to drink and eat. That's why I usually do not have much energy to respond to emails.

All right, dear sister, I guess you must be tired today as well. Please sleep and rest well. May our Lord comfort you in His soft arms.

May Lin

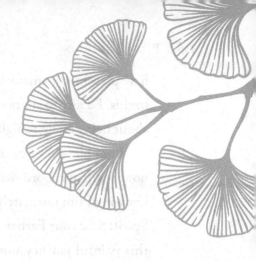

Chapter 3
BEING ALONE

He went off to the mountain to pray, and He
spent the whole night in prayer to God.
—Luke 6:12

April 7

My dear treasured sister Torie,

What an honor and a privilege to know that
I could be as comforting to you as you are to me
by sharing my story or my heart with you. In this
life's journey, you and I have had a lot of *being-alone*
moments, respectively, but I could see from you,
from me, that our Father reveals His tender care
toward us, and through our experience, we will
witness to the world.

Your being-alone moments with God—
through your journal and through your emails—

have presented so many insights. In corresponding to this, I'd love to share with you what I just wrote about being alone tonight.

I am blessed to be able to be alone every day now with our Lord with new, seeing eyes and knowing Him intimately by the work of the Holy Spirit. Since our Father allowed me to go through this painful journey under physical, mental, and spiritual shocks, I feel like I have grown in my knowledge, and understanding of Him.

Right in the midst of these shocks, He is showing and teaching me not to wonder when this storm will pass but dare to meet Him right here and dance with praise and prayer with a new spirit and mind. By grace, He even opened my physical eyes to see more of His creations and hear more of His creatures' praises. Without a doubt, He revealed his heart to me in an unspoken way through His spirit and through His children like you.

Being alone, He died for me thousands of years ago. Being alone, He called me by name over twenty years ago. Being alone, ten years ago, He opened my heart. Being alone, He has been working on my spirit to be obedient, to be trustful, and to be faithful in His kingdom-building. Being alone, I realize the genuine state and condition of having this king of kings and the only one true God at my beck and call.

Right in the middle of this storm, I naturally stopped thinking about earthly things, but I ran into His arms to hide in His grace. Right in the midst of this weakness, I willingly surrender my thinking and my ways to submit in seeking His good purpose. Right in the midst of my loss, I completely gave up my will, but I let *His* will be revealed and fulfilled. Or I should say that right in the midst of this storm, He quiets all the voices bothering me that say I will not recover, so why give God praise for making me sick? But in those quiet moments, He speaks to me with His truth.

You know what, Torie, last Christmas of 2015, I spent seven days on my own fasting, reading the Bible, praying, and seeking Him. I received incredible peace in the end, and I heard a voice whisper, "May Lin, don't you believe that I will heal you?"

However, after that, my doctor's further checkup revealed that the cancer was spreading instead of stopping; however, there is peace holding me through the process now. In my heart, I need to let the Lord heal my body, my mind, and my spirit. I did not have any miraculous signs from God to validate what I experienced. But by faith, I believe

I had a divine encounter as a result of my being alone, fasting, and praying.

What shall I say, Torie? Nothing ... but praise and be thankful to our Lord for his faithfulness to keep my faith in Him, to work diligently by all means of environment, His children, and His spirit.

Being alone, He holds my breath. Being alone, He sustains my body. Being alone, He nurtures my mind. Being alone, He speaks to my spirit. He transforms my heart from this world without hope to His kingdom where hope is realized. Being alone, He is the true God. Only He is holy, pure, powerful, wise, and good.

Let's keep growing in His grace, my dear strong cheerful sister Torie!

May Lin

April 15

Dear May Lin,

The Lord wakes me in the early morning hours so our time together is quiet and uninterrupted. The cool fresh air of each new day reminds me that no matter what happened the day before, God gives us a fresh start, a new day, a reaffirmation of God's handiwork as I watch the sun rise and the moon fade away from night duty. The birds chirp their morning greeting and the dew gives everything a glittering sheen. It was like something out of the story of Snow White. "Disneyland, eat your heart out!"

June 8

My dear sister and friend Torie in Christ,

Thank you for your text message yesterday; sorry I did not get back to you due to my tiredness. But feel better today and love to share with you my updates in the past weeks as well as some of my personal Bible study as follows.

Romans 8:28 is so deep in God's promise and love, which He uses to test us how much we know Him and how eager we need to seek Him. I also like this verse in the NLT version, which is translated as "God causes everything to work together for the good of those who love God and are called according to His purpose for them."

The action of God's "causes" is so powerful and so comforting for me to realize who is in real charge of everything happening in my life, which is far beyond my own determination and decision, which only causes me to turn to Him constantly, to know Him better, to trust Him a bit more.

As His creation, unless He chooses to teach us by His spirit, we would never be able to know Him, to acknowledge His nature and character, and to understand why he selected us for a special calling. For myself, I see clearly that unless a big tragedy happens to blow my mind away, I won't be able to learn, to let myself go, to start submitting myself to His hand, and as my human nature could still deceive me, to control and hold on to planning things on my own, which separates me from the wonderful work of God and from the true glory I can give to the Lord as His vessel.

Only Christ can save us from the power of sin; however, he also exchanges our old life for a new life with Him. His spirit dwells in us and leads us in our work constantly. Even our faith in Him is not our own doing. It is part of God's salvation; that's truly a gift from God.

This cancer is an awakening point that God uses to get me to pay attention to His words and to listen to Him in my own poverty. These are:

1. poverty of wisdom,
2. poverty of obedience, and
3. poverty of power, through which He shows me His wisdom, His faithfulness, and His love.

Let us keep seeking, keep searching, keep knocking with no giving up on Him. As what He starts, He will finish for us beyond what we could think as He is working on what God is thinking. And thank you for your sincere prayers. Here is my current treatment status.

This is the sixth week of external treatment of radiation. The main side effects are as follows:

+ diarrhea, which is out of control and happens right after Monday (having chemo and radiation that day);
+ poor sleep;
+ nausea caused by the above;
+ hemorrhoids; and
+ kidney pain.

Next week, I will have a planning day to locate the internal treatment place for my doctor. Then, I will have three weekly internal treatments of radiation. In the meantime, my doctor may start another three courses of chemo overlapping that.

+ By God's provision, I still have something to drink such as rice soup, chicken soup, and nutrition shakes, which maintain my body's needs.
+ By God's strength, I still can walk every day no matter how I feel.

41

- By God's grace, I am able to accept treatment after weekly blood tests, even though some items of my blood dropped out of range.
- By God's leading, I keep coming back to His Word's study and He brings other Christians to come to us, to pray with us.
- By God's love, I see more limitations of my own nature and more of the Lord's unlimited nature.

I miss you too and have been remembering you and your trip in our daily prayers, and I look forward to our next meeting.

Hugs with His Love,
May Lin

June 9

Last night I received another email from May Lin. As usual, her words stirred up a bundle of emotions. Her praise and worship of God in these trying circumstances is a model we should follow when times are rough and the future looks bleak. I know something wrong is going on in my own body, but God is faithful by giving me May Lin as an example of faith to follow.

June 13 (later in the day)

My dear sister Torie,

Thank you very much for your beautiful sharing, encouragement, and opening through these two emails sent over to me. I love your analogy of the crawling caterpillar on my current tough journey though I have no idea how long this will take. Thinking about the soaring butterfly does light up my heart to look up, to look forward, and to look at life with *hope*.

Also, when I read your words, "I realize the heights of spiritual insight and an awareness God has given you, and I hunger for it," I feel the opposite about myself. Frankly, from all your stories, all your actions, all your sharing, I actually hunger for the love, the passion, the dedication the Holy Spirit has given you toward the Lord Christ.

To be honest, my limited sharing with you and other brothers and sisters are very few times that the Word of God has enlightened me or lifted my spirit like the light cracked into a thick cold dark cave. However, in front of God, I have to admit that I do not have your love, your passion, and your dedication to the Lord, which I do desire to have. I pray that the Holy Spirit will reveal the truth worthy of the Lord's resurrected life to me and that my own eyes could be open to the truth.

When I was baptized in 2005, I only experienced freedom from the shame and guilt of my sins through the acceptance of the blood of Christ on the cross. I believe that's the work of the Holy Spirit, to reveal such valuable truth to set me free. Yet, recently, I come to realize that I never fully experienced the resurrected new life of Christ dwelling inside me, with which I dare to pour out all of myself and all my dearest people or things I treasured in this world for Him. Seems like something is hindering that true new life from flowing through me, without which I always feel so dissatisfied.

June 14

Amen and amen, my sister Torie, for what you shared and revealed by God's words. Even though in my current situation, it seems my world is pretty small, and I even get isolated from this world, God never stops His work and His will in me and in this life. I see one thing clearly: because of this cancer, I am getting more real with myself and with the people around me on this journey. This realness has happened in my brokenness, or shall I say, by the waking up from the Lord to help distinguish what is real in Him, in me, in this life, in this world.

Though I am not very happy and satisfied and understanding about His timing of His revelation to me, to Ken, to you; this never stops His way, His glory, His work, His truth. It's me who needs patience with my Father, our God, our Lord, our *winner*!

This cancer is only an eye-opener to see my spiritual condition.

June 15

My dear beloved May Lin,

Upon rising from bed this morning, you were on my mind. I played my favorite song, "All the Earth" by the Parachute Band. As I listened, I looked out in my backyard. The sun has returned illuminating and giving sparkle to all the effects of the rain. Everything is so green and all the colors are so vibrant. I am sending you the words of the song. Read them and breathe them in deeply, calling on your spirit to internalize the words for you. Does it give you a lift as it did me? When I first opened my Bible, it fell open to the very words of this song. I knew instantly that the Lord was validating my feelings regarding the words of the song. Here are some of the words from the Bible which are in the song.

Psalm 95:1–2 (NIV), "Let us come before him with thanksgiving and extol him with music and song. Sing to the Lord a NEW SONG; sing to the Lord, all the earth, Sing to the Lord, praise his name; proclaim his salvation day after day."

Psalm 96:11–13, "Let the heavens rejoice, let the earth be glad; let the sea resound, and all that is in it; let the fields be jubilant, and everything in them. Then all the trees of the forest will sing for joy; they will sing before the Lord, FOR HE COMES!"

Please don't feel like you have to answer my emails. It is enough to know that you can read them or have Ken read them to you. I truly believe they are fed to me by God as a way He wants to encourage you and reveal his love. Whatever you are suffering now, please know that you are greatly loved.

I know from what God is allowing me to endure now, that in my greatest moments of weakness, He is creating a *new song* in me. He plants poetry in the furrows of my mind in the middle of the night that screams for release until I get up and write them down. The words flow like a waterfall. Some time I will share them with you.

But for now, I pray that these words from God will soothe your wounds and make merry your heart.

In His perfect love,
Torie

June 16

Dear May Lin,

I fear your treatments are so debilitating that you are not able to respond to my emails. It's OK. I wish I could visit you; however, I've been having many doctor appointments to try and figure out why I am having so much pain in my limbs. It is not all arthritis but something else. It's also hard for me to concentrate and verbalize my thoughts. Writing is no problem, so I am content to lose myself in my writings.

Allow me to share with you a poem that I wrote recently.

The Lord Is My Gardener

The Lord is my gardener
I am His seed.
He uses His gardening tools to
Shovel deep into the soil of my heart

Hoes furrows into a soft bed to lie in
Spades dirt to cover me gently with
The topsoil of His protection
Fertilizes me with His word of Truth
Hoes away encroaching weeds of deception
Sprinkles living water over me, like prayers
Sprays away insects and diseases
The devils of destruction
Prunes with shears to shape my branches of faith
To grow a strong stem of Christlike character
Harvests my fruit to share the sweetness of his grace
Fruit that bears more seeds so the orchard grows
Our fruit to serve at the heavenly wedding feast
The Gardener is pleased. He proudly declares
"Well done, my good and faithful servant!"

Again, I am drawn to the attributes of nature to express the attributes of God and His dealings with us. With all the evidence pointing to a divine creator, why can't people believe?

Do the trees go through a seasonal change of their own accord? Does the Earth rotate and revolve around the sun on its own power? Do flowers bloom from seeds without assistance? Does a baby know its mother's breast by instruction? And does the moon at night, and the sun at day decide their own position at the right time?

Is a poem written without the inspiration of a poet? From whom does love come from? Is it born of itself without a heart as its chamber? Can love awaken itself without an object of affection? Or can we share a love for one another without demonstration?

The whole order of things screams God.

Chapter 4

BORN WORLDS APART, UNITED AS ONE IN CHRIST

For by one Spirit we were all baptized into one body,
whether Jews or Greeks, whether slaves or free.
—1 Corinthians 12:13

June 17

Good morning, dear sister May Lin,

I find it amazing that we are truly sisters by the appointment of our Lord. Born worlds apart, speaking different languages, influenced by completely different cultures and traditions, inheriting the fallout from different kinds of oppression and hardships, differences in our appearances, differences, differences.

Yet we are the *same* as *one* in Christ.

Paul says in Galatians 1:15 (NIV), "God, who set us apart from birth and called me by his grace."

Unbeknown to us, before our first breath, our first thought, our first heartbeat, our God of Sovereignty united us together as sisters as though we were knitted together in the same womb.

Every path we have walked has led us to be together at this appointed time for His appointed purpose. What are the odds of that happening as a coincidence?

To prove further that his transformation was of God and not by any other influences of the world or man, Paul did not go to Jerusalem for validation but went to Arabia (alone) for three years. Imagine, if we would have spent three years alone with God praying and keeping our ears open to his spirit speaking to us, the impact that would have made in our lives. But God (and I believe Paul did also) knew that the work that He was assigned to Paul would require incredible renewal (a regeneration) of his mind and spirit. God had to make him "a new creation" in Christ, dying to the old self, being reborn in the newness of life.

May Lin, it was not my choice to read these particular scriptures this morning. I prayed and just opened my Bible to find the place where I had left off yesterday in my study. But these scriptures were underlined from a previous reading, and they grabbed my attention today.

For this reason, the Lord wanted to make a point to both of us. I believe He is telling us that we are experiencing this time of illness as a way to place our focus on God as Paul did. Our past lives testify that we had nothing in common, which would have brought us together at this time. Just like Paul, in his sinful life, had nothing in common with the apostles. Indeed, he was pursuing their lives to put a stop to the work that was out of line with the traditional Jewish faith. His single goal was to *destroy* "the way."

In our former state, God saw that we needed that same kind of renewal and regeneration of the Holy Spirit. The fact that we were already Christians gave us assurances of our salvation but did that prepare us to obey and embrace the next phase of our spiritual development for the work He had (and still has) in mind for us to do, if needed, in a sacrificial way?

At the beginning stage, could we have truly shared in the sufferings of Christ for the sake of the gospel? I realize now that I cannot just rest on the laurels of my past work. If the seeds that were planted during that work are to grow and bring forth a rich harvest; then we, too, must also grow

53

(as the seed does) to produce beautiful flowers or fruit.

From my perspective, these insights are true. Our union, as sisters in Christ and coworkers in these circumstances, gives us the advantage of approving what each of us is receiving from God from different perspectives. Like Jonathan and David, God united them with brotherly love that went beyond friendship.

The fact that these insights are coming at such rapid speed indicates to me that there is urgency in what God wants us to do. Do you agree? Are you receiving these same types of messages? There are several ways to validate our impressions. By:

- seeking wisdom in the Word,
- praying scripturally,
- looking at our circumstances,
- becoming aware of the nudges of the Holy Spirit (He will not leave us alone until we comply), and
- the like-mindedness of fellow believers.

I am resting better these days by the serenade of the crickets at night and the chirpings of birds at dawn. Through my open bedroom window, the crickets are the last things I hear at night, and the birds are the first things I hear in the morning.

The air is fresh signifying it is "a new day the Lord has made. Let us rejoice and be glad in it."

God speaks to us in many different ways. Through the order of His creation and its perpetual commitment to carry on, no matter what chaos the world of man is experiencing; we can have peace of mind knowing God attends to His people as He attends to His creation. We are to carry on as well. These are the things that set us apart from the rest of the world.

Forgive me if reading this message tires you out. I hope it restores the hope and the confidence that God loves you, May Lin, just the way you are. Your praises and worship of Him through this illness are like the lovely fragrance of lavender. I can visualize His smile as he ties our prayers together with a ribbon of gold and inhales deeply the fragrance of our devotion to Him. In return, you can breathe in what He exhales: His blessings of love and healing.

I pray you will be remembered like the woman with the alabaster jar. She poured out the very expensive perfume to anoint the head and feet of her Savior.

What kind of love is this that she gave the most precious gift she had, the most expensive gift, in great humility to worship and praise her king amidst the ridicule and scorn of others who were more concerned with the money and thus, blinded to the value of her gift?

Have a wonderful day in the knowledge of knowing our praises of Him are a pleasing aroma to our Lord and Savior, Jesus Christ.

Wrapped in His loving arms,
Torie

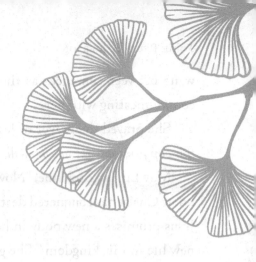

Chapter 5
REFINER'S FIRE

> He will sit as a refiner and purifier of silver.
> —Malachi 3:3

July 3

I visited May Lin yesterday, grateful that God gave us this time together. The May Lin I saw yesterday was different from the May Lin who writes me emails. It's interesting that sometimes what we write is what we hope for, but being with her in person, I saw the fear and anxiety in her face. It was easy to hide her pain behind the pen; but much harder to conceal it in person.

In my arrogance, I thought I was helping May Lin, but in reality, she was helping me with her encouragement and support. With each visit and message, I witness a closer reliance on God. She teaches me lessons of spiritual value. When she prays, her voice is soft, barely above a whisper. But her words are powerful praising God, thanking him for his blessings in an unhurried fashion. She waits between sentences as though listening to the Holy Spirit communicating with her.

She prayed the prayer of Jesus. *"Father, if you are willing, take this cup from me, yet not my will, but yours be done."*

May Lin later told me, "Now I have no fear of dying because I know Christ has conquered death. Our bodies are only temporary. Jesus promises a new body in heaven. I'm looking forward to my new life in His kingdom." She gave me a book called *Jesus Freaks Do Talk: The Voices of the Martyrs*. There is no room in my spirit for depression when I read the stories of these precious saints. Standing their ground of faith, they defended the Bible and their faith in Christ even if it meant torture, execution, or isolation.

On this visit with May Lin and Ken, I was shocked by how thin and pale May Lin had become. She looked so fragile as though she could be blown away by a breath of wind. She could not eat solid food now; she only drinks broth. She asked me to bring her a watermelon which I was happy to do. It was such a small request it seemed insignificant compared to what she really needed.

August 24

This morning I went back through earlier emails between May Lin and myself. I agreed with God that May Lin and I were going through a refiner's fire. Whatever was attacking my body was becoming more evident. I was growing weaker and experiencing more pain. However, I did not share the news with May Lin or Ken. I didn't want to worry them; but basically, I didn't want to face the truth myself that something was wrong.

"So that the proof of your faith, being more precious than gold which is perishable, though it is tested by fire—may be found to result in praise and glory and honor at the revelation of Jesus Christ" (1 Peter 1:7, NIV).

As May Lin was coming to the end of her chemo treatments, I came to the end of my year reading through the Bible. What had I learned? God takes us on many journeys throughout our lives. Some are wonderful; some are tragic. Walking by faith that's been tested in fire will help us over the ruts and stones of conflict along the road. And when we come to the end of ourselves, then we are ready for God to use us as we travel the roads He has laid out for us.

However, journeys end, and in my experience, God already has a new journey set up and waiting for me. His plan will be accomplished—His way and in His timing.

Indeed, it's not a matter of what we want. God knows what is best for each of us.

Experiencing the power of God along the way makes our experiences so incredible that people may acknowledge them as miracles, so God gets all the glory. To the extent of our faith, so will be the things we can accomplish for Him.

So it didn't surprise me that in church the following Sunday's message was on faith. The Lord made sure his message got through to me.

"Faith is the assurance of things hoped for, the evidence of things not seen" (Hebrews 11:1).

I learned about faith in that little lot in the woods. I saw God's faithfulness every fall when the geese flew south for the winter in perfect formation and returned in spring. When my dad planted seeds in the garden, we knew they would grow. I could tell what season it was by just sniffing the air. Looking back, I can see God's providential handprint on every aspect of my life. And He's got His hand on you too, May Lin. He always rewards faith according to His perfect will.

We are in His love together,
Torie

Chapter 6
LESSONS IN WAITING

You too be patient; strengthen your hearts,
for the coming of the Lord is near.
—James 5:8

August 25

May Lin sent me her doctor's appointment dates for September—a month of testing, evaluating scans, and X-rays to see if there is any hint of cancer left in her body. Waiting is excruciating when your life is on hold.

Heavenly Father, I praise You for supporting us through the entire trauma caused by cancer when it entered May Lin's body. We don't understand why You allowed her to get sick, but we have learned to lean on Your promises for healing. You are a Sovereign God who knows what's best for us. I thank You for allowing me to be a support for May Lin and Ken during this time. I thank You for all the insights into Your Word—a cradle of comfort and love. Now, Lord, we humbly bow before You and ask for Your best for May Lin. I pray for Your blessings now by giving May Lin a clean bill of health through the examination of these tests.

"I know the plans I have for you ... plans to prosper you and not to harm you, plans to give you hope and a future" (Jeremiah 29:11). Whatever the test results show, we have confidence that You will bring good out of it.

Father, while we cannot fully fathom the extent of your grace, we believe "through Christ, we can fly on wings like eagles and move mountains." Our obedience is to bring you glory and honor. Amen!

From experience, I know that God does not take something away unless He replaces it with something new. A good illustration of that was when my mother died on June 25, 1963.

She was thirty-seven years old, and I was fourteen. Her death, heartbreaking as it was, opened the door for my escape from my father's grieving alcoholic stupors to start a new life in California.

In November 1963, I felt my heart surge against the pressure of the plane as it took off from Baltimore and soared above the clouds flying me to California. I was going to live with my aunt in San Diego. I knew then the Lord had heard my prayers. He was giving me a new beginning in life. Even being alone and underage, I was not afraid to make the journey by myself. Giddy would better describe it. I was flying high that day but not because of the plane. God was with me just like He had been through all my years living in the woods.

My aunt was very strict, and she made sure I kept good grades. Sundays were for church no matter how late I was out the night before. She found me jobs, so I could contribute to my support. It wasn't easy. I'd never been disciplined before. In Maryland, I had failed in school and finally had just stopped attending altogether.

But my aunt made me strong, and God knew that I needed discipline to succeed in what would be required of me for His future plans.

So my point, dear May Lin, is that God will provide just the right circumstances with just the right people at the right time. Although we may not be able to see the light at the end of the tunnel, He can. He will reward our waiting.

September 7

Dear brothers and sisters in Christ,

Attached are some pics taken yesterday during the "Relay of Life" organized by the American Cancer Society (ACS) in our area. The people I met there had survived cancer for a number of years, some for twenty years or more. I was very encouraged by their stories of survival. Next year, I pray I can come back and tell my story of healing.

Per ACS, I am a seven-month-old survivor. And it's amazing even to realize that I could be here to participate. Last April, our loving Pastor George and his wife Michelle invited Ken and me to participate in the Relay for Life, which they have been involved in and around their area for years. Yet honestly, at that time, I did not have any energy even for regular conversation and no desire to be exposed to the public. Now, by grace, I can stand and walk in such an event to remember to celebrate, to experience, and to be thankful.

So thank you, our faithful compassionate family, for all your thoughts, prayers, and the help you gave to Ken and me during this past year. As we shared our hearts as *one* in the spirit of our Lord, I deeply appreciate your true companionship which you devoted to us on this journey of trials and new discovery.

I have two more chemotherapies to go. Then I will have another CT scan to see whether the cancer is gone. Frankly, uncertainty is a scary thing. When I walked in the silent candle walk with other people last night (cancer patients, families, friends, and volunteers) to commemorate all cancer patients, I could not help thinking that I might be walking the path of death.

Actually, I realized I am walking on the path of death in this world even if I don't have cancer. Oddly, I had not thought about this and was unwilling to face such reality. I had been wearing my rosy-colored glasses and even subconsciously pursued something unreal in this world with vanity.

Being broken, being emptied, being poured out is a painful process, but it's the beginning to

see, hear, and feel something real and valuable with
true heart and spirit.

Maybe, you will agree with me that I came to
realize that in this world, I am walking through
death; however, I am alive in Him as He is true
life.

Love by faith in Christ,
May Lin

September 8

Dearest May Lin,

Thank you for your update and pictures of the
Walk for Life. It's thrilling that you were able to
participate in a rigorous activity. It helps to meet
people who have gone through or are going through
what you are experiencing. You have grown so
much spiritually, a huge inspiration for me and
others who will hear your story. Let me know if
you would like me to visit you this weekend.

Heavenly Father and our Lord Jesus Christ,

You have proven faithful in answering our prayers
for May Lin. We are truly grateful for Your favor
upon May Lin and Ken at this time. We have rested
in Your comfort and care through the most difficult
of times. I praise You that May Lin is coming to the

end of her treatments for this cancer. Please, Lord Jesus, carry her through the rest of the way. I recognize the growth in May Lin by drawing near to You and trusting You more. Her words of insight have been profound and could only have been initiated by the Holy Spirit. Through her, I have reaped the benefit of Your teachings, Your wisdom, and Your assurances. Praise You, Lord, for allowing me to share this journey with May Lin. It's been a tremendous blessing!

So, Father, I pray the treatment she had today will not make her sick, weak, or painful. Give her an appetite to eat and a peaceful rest at night to make her body strong. Through these treatments and the care of good doctors provided by You, I ask that every cancer cell in her body has been eliminated. I pray this time when she sees the doctor, he will realize that it is by Your power, May Lin is healed. Use her testimony to glorify Yourself and to win others to Christ. Let the world know that You are God, and there is no other. You give life and take life away. We look forward, dear Lord, to the plans you have for her and me in the days ahead. We are your faithful servants.

Protect us from the enemy. He has lost this battle! We eagerly wait to enter Your kingdom so we can hear the praises of angels and with all the saints singing for Your praise and honor. But until that time comes to pass, fit us up with the heavenly attire of light, truth, and wisdom for discernment.

For thine is the kingdom, the power, and the glory forever and ever! Help us, Father, to get a jump start on heaven by empowering us to declare the riches of Your glory and grace right here now.

Love,

Torie

Chapter 7

VICTORY AT LAST

I can do all things through Christ who strengthens me.
—Philippians 4:13

September 8

Dear loyal sister Torie,

So glad to hear from you. Thank you very much
for your fearless and sincere prayers for me in the
trust and faith of our Lord. Praise Him because
tomorrow will be my last chemo treatment. What
a journey I never expected to take in my life. But
it has been an awakening call to pursue the true
meaning of life and the true love of Christ. I thank
our Father for His faithfulness in holding me up
in His arms. And thank you for holding me up in
your prayers.

September 12

5:24 p.m.

Hallelujah! Dear family in Christ, Ken and I just got back from the doctor's visit, who excitingly shared the great news with us that per my last Friday's CAT scan and MRI reports, everything is good. *No more cancer!* It has been almost a year since I first went to the doctor in pain. I could not have imagined going through everything I have experienced this last year, back then. I am glad God only gives us a flashlight view of our future. Otherwise, I would not have been able to face such a test.

Love,
May Lin

5:52 p.m.

Oh, May Lin, I am sooooooo happy!
Thank you, Lord and Savior! You heard our cries and wiped away our tears. Praise You, praise You! Glory to You forever and ever! May Lin and I look forward to the plans You have for us.
I hope I can see you, dear sister, on Saturday. But if not, I'll try to make it the following week.

I can't wait to hold your *whole healed* body in my arms, and we will dance for the glory of Christ!

Love you always,
Torie

11:36 p.m.

Amen, my precious sister Torie! You are definitely part of His glory in this journey, standing firmly together. God is with us! You never stopped praying every day. He is guiding you in His way exclusively designed for you with His love. For your information, there is a Chinese Christian family who will stop by to visit me this Saturday on their way to the Grand Canyon. I do not mind if you join us at all. If you still don't feel well enough to come, kindly take your time as we surely can make it the following week.

Hugging you in His grace!
May Lin

September 13

If I have learned nothing else during this experience, I now have a better understanding of the deep suffering of former saints. Jesus set the example of how to suffer and how to pray in faith for the Father to heal us. But more important than the physical healing is the spiritual healing. We are healed from the inside out. We can be sure the Lord will have a new beginning and a new assignment waiting for us.

Chapter 8
OUR HOPE AND FUTURE

> Those who wait for the LORD will regain their
> strength; they will mount up with wings
> like eagles, they will run and not get tired,
> they will walk and not grow weary.
> —Isaiah 40:31

No amount of suffering is greater than the sufferings of Christ. It's scary. It's painful.

It's refining like walking through a blazing fire; however, we will come out of it as pure as gold. The reflection of His glory will shine more brilliantly to penetrate the darkest corner of the world. May Lin's confirmation of healing yesterday encouraged me to fill up at the gas station of faith each time I am traveling in uncharted territories.

There is no shortage of people suffering in this sinful world. I've witnessed horrible conditions of poverty, famine, violence, and neglect, especially in third-world countries. I saw a boy begging in the streets of Cairo with a missing hand. I learned his father had cut it off so people would feel sorry for him and give him more money while begging. Under whatever circumstances, people suffer from disease, famine, violence, and neglect because we live in a fallen world that has rebelled against God.

As Christians, God has equipped us to help others in need and love them into the faith. The Bible gives us many examples of people suffering, especially those loved by God.

Every believer goes through trials and testing in order to mature our faith and have a closer relationship with the Lord as a result. It is the *refiner's fire* that makes a difference in how we live our lives and the impact we will have on others. We are tested every day we live in the world.

This story about May Lin's miracle healing had lain quietly forgotten within the pages of my 2016 journal until now. It's in my journals that I have indulged my love for writing by keeping track of God's faithfulness throughout the years of my life.

I have greatly benefitted from the stories I've read over the years from other Christians. Their testimonies have brought light into many of my dark days. Walk through a hospital or a nursing home, and it's easy to see the loneliness and destitution many of the patients are experiencing. The best medicine is to give them the gift of our time building relationships, so the gospel message can bring them comfort and hope that is everlasting.

The sickness I was experiencing in the story was the onset of fibromyalgia. It's been hard to accept this condition after living such an active life. It's easy to ask why God would make me so sick now that I'm retired, and I have all the means and time to travel and be a witness to fulfill the great commission Jesus gave us before He went to heaven.

Didn't Paul ask the same question?

The Bible encourages us to write down our testimonies. Perhaps, God feels it's time to add another letter of recommendation to His archives of eyewitnesses, so the gospel message will be presented with a new sense of urgency during these days of the coronavirus.

While we are grateful for May Lin's healing, we are also fully aware of thousands of people who have not been healed. This book is written for the encouragement and hope of all those cancer patients still waiting for the gift of healing.

But whether it's cancer or some other life-threatening disease, the formula for healing begins with the gospel message and validating its truth by the way we live our lives.

"You yourselves are our letter, written on our hearts, known and read by everyone. You show that you are a letter from Christ, the result of our ministry, written not with ink but with the Spirit of the living God, not on tablets of stone but on tablets of human hearts" (2 Corinthians 3:2–3).

February 12, 2023

It has been seven years since May Lin experienced cancer. I wasn't sure if she wanted her story written for the world to see or if she wanted to keep it private and personal.

However, when we spoke, she not only gave me permission but was excited about the book.

Nothing much has changed in her private life, but the best news is that the cancer has not returned. She still gets checkups three times a year, but so far, she's been cancer-free.

May Lin has learned to drive, so she said this time she would come visit me. I look forward to that visit so we can continue where we left off in our relationship. Now, we have even more reason to celebrate!

EPILOGUE

THE KERITH RAVINE

Hide in the Kerith Ravine.
—1 Kings 17:3

As God's servants, we must obey His command to rest as much as He commands us to work. God demonstrated a need for rest when He set aside a rest day called, the Sabbath.

Some Christians are workaholics and are driven to work overtime, thinking they are doing more for God. However, the Bible does not support that thought.

In 1 Kings 17:1–6, Elijah said to Ahab, "As the LORD, the God of Israel, lives, whom I serve, there will be neither dew nor rain in the next few years except at my word."

Elijah would be used by God to perform eight amazing miracles in 1 and 2 Kings. God recognized that His servant would need physical and spiritual refreshment and rest.

"God's servants must be taught the value of the hidden side of life. The person who is to serve in a lofty place before others must also assume a lowly place before God. We should not be surprised if God occasionally says to us, 'Dear Child, you have had enough of this hurried pace, excitement, and publicity. Now I want you to go and hide yourself—hide in the Kerith Ravine of sickness, the Kerith Ravine of sorrow, or some place of total solitude, from which the crowds have been turned away'" (L. B. Cowman, *Streams in the Desert*).

When God calls us to service, He will first test us through "the Refiner's Fire" (Malachi 3:2). Through our brokenness and humility, God refines us through the difficulties of our lives.

In my own experience, before I answer God's calling to a new mission or work, I need to go someplace quiet alone and pray. Acquiring spiritual power can only be obtained by the filling of the Holy Spirit. Fasting and praying speed up the process. Then God knows I'm serious about my obedience to Him.

When we examine the lives of Jesus, Paul, Peter, and the other disciples, they all suffered.

"Stephen, a man full of God's grace and power, did great wonders and miraculous signs among the people" (Acts 6:8).

He was stoned to death and martyred as many of our missionaries have been martyred. If we are called on to be martyred for the Lord, "are we ready?"

Through May Lin's cancer and my fibromyalgia, we have learned to rest under the protective wings of God. He is our Kerith Ravine. Since that year of testing, we've come out stronger and more equipped to follow Him wherever He leads us to go.

The End

Printed in the United States
by Baker & Taylor Publisher Services

Printed in the United States
by Baker & Taylor Publisher Services